Penguin
Random
House

Recipe Writer and Food Stylist
Kate Turner

Writer and Editor Ruth O'Rourke-Jones

Project Art Editor Harriet Yeomans

Editorial Assistant Alice Horne

Design Assistance
Jade Wheaton, Alison Gardner

Jacket Designer Harriet Yeomans

Jacket Coordinator Libby Brown

Pre-Production Producer
Rob Dunn

Print Producer Stephanie McConnell

Creative Technical Support
Sonia Charbonnier

Photography Will Heap

Managing Editor Dawn Henderson

Managing Art Editor
Marianne Markham

Art Director Maxine Pedliham

Publishing Director Mary-Clare Jerram

US Managing Editor Kayla Dugger

US Publisher Mike Sanders

First American Edition, 2017
Published in the United States by
DK Publishing, 345 Hudson Street,
New York, New York 10014

Copyright © 2017 Dorling Kindersley Limited
DK, a Division of Penguin Random House LLC
17 18 19 20 21 10 9 8 7 6 5 4 3 2 1
001–304992–February/2017

A catalog record for this book is available
from the Library of Congress.

ISBN 978-1-4654-6229-9

DK books are available at special discounts when purchased
in bulk for sales promotions, premiums, fund-raising, or
educational use. For details, contact: DK Publishing Special
Markets, 345 Hudson Street, New York, New York 10014
SpecialSales@dk.com
Printed and bound in China

All images © Dorling Kindersley Limited
For further information see: www.dkimages.com

A WORLD OF IDEAS:
SEE ALL THERE IS TO KNOW
www.dk.com

MY
ZERO-
WASTE
KITCHEN

Contents

NOW ZERO-WASTE IT!

Zero waste:
what's it all about?

Going "zero waste" means trying to live a more sustainable life. It is a goal to aspire to and your kitchen is the perfect place to start. Having a zero-waste kitchen means buying less food in the first place, reusing whatever you can, however you can, and throwing less away. Don't worry, you won't have to completely overhaul your whole lifestyle—in fact, you might just be surprised at the big difference some small, simple changes can make. From planning your grocery shopping to what you put on your plate,

this book is full of amazing tips and tricks to help you get creative, start reducing waste, and even have fun doing it!

The three "Rs"

Key to zero-waste living are the three "Rs:"

REDUCE • REUSE • RECYCLE

"Reduce" means not buying more than you need and this is where a little planning goes a long way. "Reuse" means making the most of those leftovers rather than trashing them. With

Swap-it smoothie p12

Creative chips p46

Hero hummus p20

a bit of thought and inspiration you can turn your "waste" foods into delicious meals that are good for you, for your wallet, and for the planet! Try the recipes in this book as a starting point and soon you'll be experimenting with whatever you have on hand. Finally, "recycle" anything that you can't reduce or reuse. Throughout this book you'll find inspirational, easy, and imaginative ways to put all these ideas into practice and help you on your zero-waste journey.

shake up your cake p58

" *A few* small **changes** *can make a* **big** *difference.* "

Getting started
no more waste!

Going ZERO-WASTE is easy—with a little thought and planning, you'll soon be on your way. Stopping to consider WHAT you throw away and WHY is the best place to start.

STOP! *BEFORE YOU BANISH THAT "WASTE" TO THE TRASH, ASK YOURSELF...*

CAN YOU EAT IT?

NO

CAN YOU REUSE IT?

NO

YES

Eat and enjoy!
You might be surprised—lots of things we throw away are edible (see pp.28–29).

YES

So use it again!
Many kitchen items can be revived, reused, or repurposed (see pp.68–69).

Foil trays

Dry-cured meats

Hard cheese

ALL DONE!

CLEVER COMPOSTING

Composting is one of the best ways to go zero-waste. It puts the energy that goes into producing food back into the soil in your garden. In a compost bin, microbes use air and water to break down organic matter into nutrient-rich dirt.

All you need is a bin that lets air circulate. Start with a leaf layer (shredded paper will do), then add fruit and vegetable scraps, and water. Add to your compost year-round. Stir it occasionally and in 8–9 months you'll have natural fertilizer.

A countertop composter helps you compost as much as you can. Put scraps into your mini composter through the week and add them to your garden compost once it's full. Use a proper container to avoid attracting flies into your kitchen!

Countertop composter

CAN YOU COMPOST IT?

NO

CAN YOU RECYCLE IT?

NO

YES

Add to your composter.
You can compost much more than you may realize (see pp.16–17)!

Scraps

YES

Put it in the recycling bin.
Up to 60 percent of waste that ends up in landfill could have been recycled! Check before you chuck!

THROW IT IN THE TRASH.

YOU'RE A WASTE-FREE WINNER!

Recycling bin

Store it right!

*Storing your produce in the **RIGHT WAY** can be the difference between **MAKING THE MOST** of your food and throwing it **OUT**.*

Where should I store it?

Check labels when you put your shopping away as many products carry storage instructions.

Once opened, some items need to go in the fridge (see p.48) and be used within a few days, so note when you open the package. Store salad items and leafy greens in the salad drawer of your fridge. If your fruits need to ripen before eating, don't chill them, leave them out in a fruit bowl until they are ready. Your kitchen pantry is great for shutting out light so keep spices, oils, and some vegetables—such as onions and root vegetables—dry and dark, in here.

What should I put it in?

Reusable containers do a great job of cutting down on waste.

Using the right containers keeps your food in tip-top condition for as long as possible. Transfer dried goods, such as spices or pasta and rice, to airtight glass or ceramic jars to keep them fresh for 6 months or more. While plastic is easy to carry around for food-on-the-go, it should only be used for cold food, as high tempertaures can cause it to break down. In the fridge, keep asparagus, cucumber, carrots, and celery fresh by placing them upright in a jar of water.

Super tip

Stop garlic spoiling by tying bulbs in panty hose. Then hang them up!

Be prepared!

With a little prep, some foods can be stored for much longer.

Blanching vegetables, such as green beans, before freezing them not only makes them last longer but also brightens their color and slows nutrient loss. Put them in the freezer on a baking sheet then transfer to an airtight container—they will keep for up to 10 months.

Drying vegetables, such as onions and chiles, for storage is easy. Use a dehydrator (see right) for fleshy chiles. For waxy varieties, wash them in salt water, then put them on a wire rack in a warm, dry spot—a windowsill is good. In a few weeks you will have a batch of dried chiles.

Airtight containers keep food fresh and dry.

A LiTTLE EXTRA HELP...

You don't need to use fancy gadgets and gizmos to go zero-waste but some ingenious inventions can help.

- **A dehydrator** is handy for preserving fruit, vegetables, herbs, and even meat. It gently dries food out while preserving nutrients and flavor.

- **Vacuum-packing** your food preserves freshness by removing air and saves valuable space.

- **A cut-herb keeper** will help your herbs stay fresher for longer by suspending them in water.

cut-herb keeper

Swap-it Smoothie

*From **APPLE CORES** to **KIWI SKINS** and **LEFTOVER GREENS**, this nutrient-packed smoothie gets the most out of your fruit and vegetables.*

SERVES 2

¾ cup fresh strawberries

¾ cup frozen berries, such as blueberries and raspberries

1½ cups nut milk, such as almond milk

¼ cup oats

2 tbsp seeds, such as hemp, chia, sesame, or flax, plus extra to garnish (optional)

1 tbsp raw honey, plus extra to taste

FIRST **MAKE THE BASE**

1 Place all the ingredients in a high-speed blender and process until smooth.

2 Add extra honey to taste and pour the smoothie into glasses to serve. Sprinkle with extra seeds to garnish, if using.

Super tip
There's no need to hull the strawberries —just add them in whole.

KIWI AND BANANA WITH SKINS

To the base recipe, add **1 small banana**—about 2½oz (75g)—with the skin on but tough ends removed, and **half a kiwi**—about 1¾oz (50g)—with the skin on.

LEFTOVER GREENS

Add about 2 handfuls of **leftover greens** such as chopped kale stalks, broccoli stems and leaves, celery tops and tails, lettuce, spinach, or avocado, to the base recipe.

OLD APPLES AND CORES

Add **1 medium unpeeled apple or apple cores**—about 4¼oz (120g)—to the base recipe. Remove the tough stalk, but keep the seeds.

Zero-waste week

Planning ahead can make the difference between a **WASTEFUL WEEK** and a **WASTE-FREE ONE**. Follow these simple pointers to help you on your way.

PLAN YOUR MEALS

Life gets in the way of the best-laid plans. If you struggle to stick to a strict meal plan, you could try planning your meals more loosely. This makes it easy to adapt as plans change. Having space to vary meals makes shopping easier and helps you waste less. Consider basing your week's evening meals around a type of food, such as pasta, fish, or grains (see meal plan, right). That way, you can stretch ingredients across a few meals and work in what you have on hand or what you feel like enjoying that day.

MEAL PLAN

Monday	Tuesday	Wednesday
RICE • stir-fry • risotto • paella • chili • curry	DOUGH • pizza • pie • quiche • fajitas	LEGUMES • soups • stews • casseroles

Friday	Saturday	Sunday
FISH • with any vegetable and mashed or boiled potatoes or potato chips	GO OFF PLAN! • eat out • invite friends for dinner • try something new	MEAT AND/OR GRAINS • Sunday roast • grain-based meatloaf and salad

RICE—Chicken & pancetta risotto

FISH—Add veggies and potatoes

DOUGH—Salmon & spinach quiche

INVOLVE EVERYONE

When it comes to planning meals for the week, get everybody involved from the start. List meals that everyone in your household enjoys and make that your starting point. You are all far more likely to stick to a meal plan that you feel enthusiastic about. You can vary the meals by working in leftovers and whatever you have on hand.

Roasted chicken

Roasted vegetables

Thursday

PASTA
- with whatever you have in your vegetable drawer
- with herb pesto

LEFTOVER LUNCHES

When planning your dinners, think about how you can use leftovers in lunches. Rather than reheating the same meals, give them a new spin. Spoon yesterday's chili into wraps, turn last night's pasta into a salad, or layer leftovers in a plastic container or glass jar.

Bean sprouts
Hummus
Beets
Peas
Boiled egg
Red peppers
Spinach
Brown rice

PASTA—Leftover vegetables

BREAK IT DOWN

You might find that planning and shopping for a whole week's worth of food doesn't work for you. If you find it hard to stick to a plan or you are wasting food toward the end of the week, try breaking your week down into a 3- or 4-day plan instead. You can then devote the following day to making meals from any leftovers you have.

LEGUMES— Bean & pumpkin soup

15

10

COMPOST

CUPCAKE LINERS

Paper cupcake or muffin liners can be added to your compost heap where they will break down quickly. Do watch out for any waxy-feeling liners that may contain an element of plastic, which you shouldn't compost. If in doubt, leave it out!

STALE SNACK FOODS

Old chips, crackers, and cookies will break down fast in a compost heap, but be sure to bury them deep within the heap as they can attract unwanted visitors to your yard.

CARDBOARD

You might be used to recycling your unwanted cardboard packaging—such as egg cartons and cereal boxes, and toilet and paper towel roll tubes—but did you know that you can rip them up and add them to your compost heap?

TISSUES AND NAPKINS

Paper tissues and napkins will break down quickly in compost. Do consider what they have been used for though. If you've been unwell and used tissues to blow your nose, for example, don't compost them as you could be adding germs to your compost.

SPICES AND HERBS

Old spices and herbs that have lost their smell and flavor can be an extra addition to your compost heap.

Your humble compost heap is full of hidden surprises! Not only can it turn your unwanted **VEGETABLE PEELINGS** into **NUTRIENT-RICH FERTILIZER**, it also works wonders with a whole host of other kitchen waste.

WINE CORKS

Don't trash that cork once you've popped it! Cork is a natural product that can be added to compost. Do watch out for synthetic corks that have been made to look like the real thing though—plastic will not break down in your compost heap.

CHEWING GUM

Whether you've chewed natural plant-based gum or a synthetic gum, both can be added to your compost. It will take a while to break down but will eventually biodegrade.

WINE AND BEER

Don't pour sour wine or flat beer down the sink, they are great for compost. Both are rich in nitrogen and beer contains yeast for good microbes to feast on. Keep an eye on the moisture levels of your compost, if it's dry then add the liquids but if it's wet add dry material too, such as shredded paper, to balance it out.

DAIRY PRODUCTS

Old milk, cream, and melted ice cream can be added to your compost in small amounts. Take care to bury them deep in your heap as they may attract pests. Mix them well with plenty of leaves to trap any odors and keep your compost balanced.

COTTON KITCHEN TOWELS AND CLOTHS

Cloths or towels that are made from 100 percent natural fibers, such as cotton or linen, can be composted. Tear them into scraps to help them break down more quickly, but they may still take a while.

17

Vegetable drawer clear-out

*Faced with a drawer full of **VEGGIES THAT NEED USING FAST?** Fear not, they won't go to waste if you follow these handy hints.*

SALAD LEAVES

• **Put salad greens** into a pan and sauté them as part of a stir-fry. This works well even if your leaves are a little wilted.

• **Blend tired leaves** into soups or smoothies for an extra dose of vitamins!

ROOT VEGGIES

• **Roast batches** of mixed root vegetables and freeze or use them in soups and stews to stock your freezer.

TOMATOES

• **Add fresh tomatoes** that are past their best to soups and pasta sauce, which both freeze well.

• **Dry out tomatoes** that are still fairly firm. If you can't use the sun, dry them in your oven on its lowest heat setting or use a dehydrator. Once dried, put them in a jar and cover them with olive oil.

• **Roast tomatoes** that are going soft— they are great squashed onto toast!

BELL PEPPERS

- **Roast any wrinkly** peppers and use them up in soups, pasta sauces, or blend them into hummus (see p.20).

- **Dice them and freeze** for using later.

- **Cut into thin slices** and add them to a frittata.

CARROTS

- **Grate carrots** and use them to make fritters. Season and mix with beaten egg and flour before frying in a little oil. Try adding cumin and fresh cilantro.

- **Revive old carrots** by slicing and steaming them, then add to a salad.

- **Bake carrots** that are past their prime in cakes and muffins (see p.66).

ZUCCHINI

- **Grate or slice zucchini**, toss lightly in oil, season to taste, then grill or roast until tender. Use in salads or sandwiches.

- **Dice and add** to soups, such as minestrone or Mediterranean vegetable.

BEETS

- **Add grated beet** to a chocolate cake or brownie mix for moistness and depth of flavor.

- **Roast beets and blend** them with yogurt, garlic, and mint for a brightly colored dip.

- **Slice, steam, and toss** into a salad. You can eat the leaves too!

Hero Hummus

Take snacking to a whole new level. OLD TOMATOES, *EXTRA AVOCADO, and* LEFTOVER BEANS *add a tasty waste-free twist to your hummus.*

MAKES ABOUT 11½oz (330g)

8½oz (240g) ready-to-eat chickpeas

1 large garlic clove, coarsely chopped

1 tbsp nut or seed butter, such as almond or sunflower

½ tsp salt

2½ tbsp lemon juice

2-4 tbsp olive oil, plus extra to serve

salt and freshly ground black pepper, to taste

To serve

1 tsp chopped fresh herb leaves and stalks, such as cilantro or parsley (optional)

½ tsp paprika (optional)

1 tsp dukkah (optional)

FIRST MAKE THE BASE

1 Place the chickpeas, garlic, nut or seed butter, salt, lemon juice, and 2 tbsp of olive oil in a food processor or blender and blend until smooth. You may need to stop the processor occasionally and push the mixture back down with a spatula.

2 Add more olive oil and/or water to reach the desired consistency, if required.

3 Season with salt and pepper to taste, then drizzle with extra olive oil and sprinkle with herbs, paprika, and dukkah, if using.

4 Serve with some crunchy veggies such as bell peppers or cucumber to dip, or store your hummus in an airtight container in the fridge for 3–4 days.

old tomatoes

NOW ZERO-WASTE iT!

LEFTOVER AVOCADO

Add **half a large avocado** at step 1 and blend with the rest of the ingredients until smooth.

LEFTOVER BEANS

Swap the chickpeas for an **equal quantity of ready-to-eat beans**, such as soaked and cooked lima beans that you haven't used, or some leftover canned cannellini beans.

OLD TOMATOES

Add about **2oz (60g) old tomatoes or leftover tomato tops and bottoms** at step 1, and blend with the rest of the ingredients until smooth.

Leftover avocado

Leftover beans

Super tip

Freeze for up to 4 months!

Eggs

Recipes often call for just one part of an egg, but you can stop making your **WHITES, YOLKS,** and **SHELLS** feel like spare parts by following these tips. Soon you'll be using up **EVERY LAST BIT!**

ADD SOME SHINE

Use your egg whites as a glaze for bread, muffins, and pastries. It adds a glossy sheen and helps to keep any grains, such as poppy or sesame seeds, in place on the crust.

THICKEN SOUPS

Adding egg yolks to soups and sauces gives them a smooth, velvety feel. Make sure to mix them in while the soup or sauce is fairly cool so that you don't end up with scrambled eggs.

DON'T HOLD THE MAYO!

Mix your yolks with a hand blender, then very gradually drizzle in oil a few drops at a time while whisking constantly. This should take around 4 minutes. Add a squeeze of lemon juice or vinegar to taste.

STAIN REMOVAL

To clean a stained tea or coffee mug, simply grind up your eggshells, put them in the mug, add some warm water, and leave to soak overnight. In the morning, the stains should have vanished!

FREEZE IT!

Freeze egg whites for up to 3 months. Once defrosted, use as normal.

Egg yolks dry out when stored, but mixing a pinch of sugar or salt with each yolk before freezing will help. Label which are sweet or savory, and adjust your recipe for any added sugar or salt.

GO NUTS!

Make candied nuts by whisking your egg whites with a little water. Mix in the nuts—almonds or pecans work well—then add cinnamon and sugar to taste. Bake on a tray in a low-heat oven for around 1 hour, turning regularly, until crisp.

FROTH IT UP

Whisk your whites and add them to your cocktails. They add froth and give your drinks a wonderfully silky texture.

EGGSHELL POWDER

Packed with micronutrients, eggshells are an awesome source of calcium! Use a small amount as a supplement—try adding ¼ tsp of powder to one large smoothie. You need about 20 eggshells to make half a small jar. Rinse well and remove any membrane before you start.

1 Preheat the oven to 350°F (180°C). Bake the shells on a tray in the oven for 10 minutes.

2 Once the shells have cooled, process them in a food processor or grind with a pestle and mortar.

3 Keep grinding until you have a fine, powdery dust. Store in an airtight container in the fridge for up to 3 weeks.

Save-it Soup

STALE BREAD, LEFTOVER GRAINS, or PASTA PIECES transform this hearty vegetable soup into a delicious zero-waste meal.

SERVES 4–6

1 tbsp olive oil, plus extra to serve

1 onion, finely chopped, about ⅔ cup

2 cloves garlic, crushed

1 carrot, finely chopped, about ¾ cup

1 celery stalk, finely chopped, about ¾ cup

1 tsp dried rosemary

a generous pinch of chili powder

14oz (400g) fresh tomatoes, chopped, or 14oz can chopped tomatoes

1 zucchini, finely chopped, about 1¼ cups

¾ cup kale leaves and stalks, finely chopped, tough stalks discarded

1¾–2 pt vegetable stock

salt and freshly ground black pepper, to taste

1¾oz (50g) Parmesan cheese, shaved (optional)

small handful basil leaves, to garnish

FIRST MAKE THE BASE

1 Heat the oil in a large, lidded pan on medium-low heat.

2 Add the onion, garlic, carrot, celery, rosemary, and chili powder, and cook gently for about 10 minutes with the lid askew, until the vegetables are soft.

3 Add the tomatoes, zucchini, kale, and stock. Bring to a boil, then reduce the heat and continue to simmer, uncovered, for about 10 minutes.

4 Season with salt and pepper to taste. Serve with a drizzle of olive oil and Parmesan shavings (if using), and garnish with fresh basil.

Super tip
keep a batch of base soup in the freezer so you always have something to add leftovers to.

LEFTOVER BEANS AND STALE BREAD

Add about **9oz (250g) leftover ready-to-eat beans,** such as cannellini or borlotti, at step 3, and top with **3½oz (100g) diced, dried bread "croutons,"** at step 4.

PARMESAN RINDS AND LEFTOVER PASTA

Add **2–3 leftover Parmesan cheese rinds** to the soup and **2½oz (75g) dried pasta** at step 3, making sure you follow the cooking time of the pasta. Alternatively, add **1⅔ cups leftover cooked pasta** toward the end of step 3 to heat through. Remove the rinds before serving.

LEFTOVER GRAINS OR PULSES

Add about **1¼ cups leftover cooked grains or pulses,** such as buckwheat, brown rice, or lentils, to your soup toward the end of step 3. Heat through before serving.

Cake pan
clear-out

What can you do with the contents of your cake pan when it's starting to **DRY OUT?** From **BAKING BISCOTTI** to **SHAKING IT UP**, try these ideas to give your cakes a second take.

FREEZE IT!

While most cakes freeze well, avoid freezing cakes that have a cream or buttercream filling. Once your cake is cool, wrap it well in foil or plastic wrap. It should keep for a few months.

TASTY TOPPING

Simply sprinkle your stale cake crumbs over ice cream for a quick and easy dessert.

SPONGE LAYER

Dry cake makes a great base for sponge-based desserts, as it absorbs any fruity juices well.

BAKE BISCOTTI

Slice up old pieces of cake and bake them in the oven at 250°F (130°C) for around 50 minutes to make crunchy biscotti or sweet croutons.

CAKE SHAKE

Cake meets milkshake in this blended sweet treat. It's a neat way of using up old cake, as the moisture from the milk more than compensates for any dryness.

— — — — — —

1 Break up dry slices of cake, such as fruitcake (see p.58), and crumble them into a food processor.

2 Pour in enough nut milk, such as almond milk (or see p.59), to cover the cake and blend until smooth.

3 Add a little more milk if you prefer a runnier shake and blend again. Sprinkle cake crumbs on top to serve.

SWEET CRUST

Dry your cake out completely by baking it at low heat. Once cool, grind into crumbs and use to make a sweet pie crust, like a cookie base.

CAKE REVIVAL

Revive stale cake by putting it in an airtight container with a slice of bread or apple overnight.

Cake shake

FRENCH TOAST CAKE

Cut thick slices of stale cake. Whisk 3 eggs with 1 cup milk in a dish. Heat butter in a pan. Dip slices in the egg mix and fry on each side until golden brown.

Check it
before you chuck it

*Knowing how to tell whether food is really **OFF** or whether it can still **BE SAVED** is not only **VITAL FOR YOUR HEALTH** but will also help you on your **ZERO-WASTE** quest!*

TEST YOUR MEAT

Smell meat to check whether it's safe to eat. Fresh meat should have little or no odor—if it smells putrid, don't eat it! Check the texture. If meat is slimy or sticky, toss it. Color is not a good guide as meats vary—changes in shade don't always mean that the meat is off.

TEST YOUR EGGS

To check an egg for freshness put it into a glass of water. If it is fresh it will drop to the bottom and rest on its side. Standing on one end at the bottom means it's a bit old but fine to eat. However, if the egg floats to the surface you should throw it away.

FRESH

OK

DON'T EAT

Bad eggs float because they have air inside them— making them less dense than water

TEST YOUR BUTTER

To check whether your butter is fresh, cut a small slice from the block and look closely at the color. The color should be the same inside as on the outside. If the inside of the butter looks lighter it has oxidized and should be thrown away. You can always freeze butter if you aren't going to use it in time.

Color should be the same inside and out

TEST YOUR OIL

Most rancid oils have a grassy or paint-like scent. Olive oil is an exception and smells like crayons when spoiled.

TEST YOUR FLOUR

Flour should have no smell at all. If your flour smells slightly sharp or bitter then it has gone off and you need to throw it away.

MOLD MATTERS

If you can see mold on the surface of food it means tiny fungi have penetrated deep inside. What you can see on top are only the spores, but their microscopic, threadlike roots will have spread throughout the food. Just scraping mold off the top will leave these roots behind. In general, this means you must throw the food away as some fungi can make you ill. However, there are a few exceptions, which are shown here.

YOU CAN STILL EAT...

Scrub off any mold

Cut away mold and 1in (3cm) around it

Cut away mold and at least 1in (3cm) below it

Dry-cured meat

Hard cheese

Hard fruit

Waste-free Frittata

Make a meal out of your leftovers. This recipe breathes life into
VEGETABLE PEELINGS, SMOKED FISH, *or Leftover* **ROASTED VEGETABLES.**

SERVES 2-4

1 tbsp coconut or olive oil

1 onion, about ½ cup, finely chopped

3 garlic cloves, crushed

1⅔ cups spinach, tough stalks removed, chopped

1½ cups broccoli florets, stem, and leaves, finely chopped

⅓ cup peas, fresh or frozen

6 eggs

⅔ cup milk, nut or dairy

2 tbsp fresh chopped herbs such as parsley, dill, chives, or thyme

2½oz (75g) cheese, such as feta or Cheddar, crumbled or grated (optional)

salt and freshly ground black pepper

FIRST MAKE THE BASE

1 Heat the oil in a medium, nonstick, ovenproof frying pan over medium heat.

2 Add the onion and garlic, and cook for 3–4 minutes until soft.

3 Add the vegetables and cook for an additional 4–5 minutes.

4 Whisk the eggs and milk together. Stir in the herbs and cheese, if using, then season with salt and pepper to taste.

5 Preheat the broiler on the medium setting.

6 Level out the vegetables in the pan and gently pour the egg mixture over them. Reduce the heat to low-medium and continue to cook the frittata for 10–15 minutes, without stirring, until the underside is cooked.

7 Place the pan under the broiler for about 5 minutes to set the top of the frittata.

8 Remove the frittata from the broiler and allow to cool for 2–3 minutes before serving.

Super tip

Leftover frittata can be stored in the fridge for 1–2 days, and is delicious eaten cold.

VEGGIE PEELINGS

Replace the spinach with 3½oz (100g) mixed vegetable peelings, such as carrot, beet, parsnip, or potato, and add to the frittata at step 3 with a splash of water. Increase the cook time at step 3 to 10 minutes.

SMOKED FISH

Add 1 cup of leftover ready-to-eat smoked fish, skinned and broken into bite-sized pieces, at step 6.

LEFTOVER ROASTED VEG

Replace the spinach, broccoli, and peas with around **10oz (300g) leftover cold roasted vegetables**. Chop into small cubes if necessary, and add to the frittata at step 3.

Tops and tails

*Don't throw away those leftover bits of **VEGETABLES**. Use them to **ADD FLAVOR** to soup or **MAKE STOCK**—in fact, the possibilities are endless!*

SHRED AND STiR

- Finely chop broccoli stalks, beet ends, and celery leaves, then add them to your stir-fries.

iT'S A WRAP

- Use up tough outer leaves of red cabbage by boiling them until they soften. They are great for wrapping food parcels or dumplings.

MASH iT UP

- Chop and sauté the tops of scallions or green onions and add them to mashed potato for a big flavor boost.

SQUASHED!

- Boil up any squash flesh trimmings, then process into a puree for a side to serve with fish.
- Roast pumpkin seeds discarded from fresh pumpkins and use them as a nutritious garnish on salad.

MIND THAT RIND

- Watermelon rind can be added to smoothies or chopped up and added to stews to help bulk them out.

Super tip

Make stock by frying vegetable tops and tails in olive oil. Add water and herbs or spices of your choice. Bring to a boil and simmer for around 15 minutes before straining through a sieve.

HERBALICIOUS

- Herb stems—such as basil, cilantro, and parsley—make a tasty addition to smoothies or chop them finely into soups and stews.

TOP SMOOTHIES

- Add strawberry tops to your smoothies for extra vitamins and fiber!

ADD SOME CRUNCH

- Liven up salads by adding crunchy raw broccoli stalks or cauliflower.

TIP TOP CARROTS

- Use green carrot tops in pesto (see p.40), or as a pretty garnish.

33

Lemons and limes

*Are you tired of wasting the parts of your lemons and limes that your recipes don't call for? Think beyond adding a slice to your drinks. Here's how to **MAKE THE MOST** of these flavorsome fruits...*

ZESTY DRESSING

Squeeze lemon or lime juice straight onto salad leaves for an instant lift. Or try mixing lime juice with an equal amount of olive oil, a crushed garlic clove, then add honey to sweeten, and season to taste.

FROZEN SLICES

Slice up leftover lemons and limes, put them onto a baking sheet, and place in the freezer. Once frozen, transfer the slices to a freezer bag ready to put in your ice-cold drinks!

DRIED SLICES

Place your lemon and lime slices on a cooling rack over a baking sheet so that air can get to both sides. Put them in the oven on low heat for around 2 hours until dry. Use them to flavor tea or chop them and add into soups.

LEMON MAYO

Adding both lemon zest and juice to mayonnaise gives it a zesty twist! Simply grate the zest into your mayo and/or squeeze in some juice, then mix it up.

CITRUS INFUSION

Use leftover citrus peel to flavor spirits, such as vodka. Simply place the peel into the bottle of vodka and leave it to infuse.

JUICE CUBES

When frozen, transfer cubes to a freezer bag. You can use them whenever you need to add fresh lemon or lime juice to a recipe. A cube should equal around 1 tbsp of juice.

CITRUS POWDER

Use up citrus peel with this zesty powder. It tastes great sprinkled over chicken or fish. You can use a dehydrator on its lowest setting and dry the peels for around 12 hours or preheat your oven to about 175°F (80°C). You will need: 5½oz (150g) leftover citrus peel, and a large pinch of salt (optional).

1 Spread the peels evenly in a single layer on a baking sheet and bake for 2–3 hours until crisp and dry.

2 Allow the dry peels to cool completely on the sheet—this takes about 10 minutes.

3 Add the salt, if using, then blend in a food processor or high-speed blender.

4 Store the dust in an airtight container in the fridge for up to 3 months.

Rescue-it Risotto

*Add **COLD CUTS**, or **LEFTOVER VEGETABLES** or **ASPARAGUS STALKS** to this pantry-stored risotto for a real supper savior.*

SERVES 2-3

1 tbsp coconut or olive oil, plus extra to serve

1 onion, finely chopped, about ⅔ cup

1 garlic clove, crushed

1 celery stalk, finely chopped, about ¾ cup

1 cup risotto rice, such as Arborio

1 qt hot vegetable or chicken stock

2oz (60g) Parmesan cheese, grated

salt and freshly ground black pepper, to taste

1 tbsp chopped parsley, to garnish

¼-½ tsp chili flakes, to garnish (optional)

FIRST MAKE THE BASE

1 Heat the oil in a large pan over medium–low heat. Add the onion, garlic, and celery, and cook, stirring occasionally, for about 5 minutes or until soft.

2 Add the rice and increase the heat to medium–high, stirring constantly for 1–2 minutes.

3 Add a ladleful of stock and stir until thoroughly absorbed into the rice.

4 Repeat this process a ladleful at a time, until the rice is creamy and tender, but still firm to the bite. Depending on your rice, this will take 15–25 minutes, and the amount of stock needed will vary.

5 Remove the pan from the heat and stir in the Parmesan cheese.

6 Season to taste with salt and pepper. Place the lid on the pan and set aside for 2–3 minutes before serving.

7 Garnish with the parsley and chili flakes, if using.

ASPARAGUS STALKS

Use up the whole of your asparagus spears. Take around 5½oz (150g) **asparagus ends** and discard any parts that are very dry. Finely slice the rest into thin "coins." Stir into the risotto with the last ladleful of stock at step 4.

LEFTOVER ROASTED CHICKEN

Shred about 5½oz (150g) cold, **leftover chicken**, discarding the skin if necessary. Add to the risotto toward the end of step 4 to heat through.

LEFTOVER VEGETABLE DRAWER VEGGIES

Use up to around 7oz (200g) **leftover mixed veggies** from your vegetable drawer, such as carrots, bell peppers, or zucchini. Chop, and then steam in a double boiler until cooked through. Add to the risotto toward the end of step 4 and continue as per the recipe.

Super *tip*

Mix all 3 variations for a zero-waste feast!

Grow it, don't throw it: lettuce

Don't throw away those **LETTUCE ENDS!** The bases can be used to grow your very own **FRESH VEGETABLES**—a great way to make the most of your "waste." Follow these simple steps to get growing!

1 Chop off any leafy parts of your lettuce that you haven't already used so that just the root base remains. Pour a little warm water into a shallow bowl.

Super tip
Cabbage and celery can also be grown using this technique!

You only need the base of the lettuce head—you can eat the rest!

CHOP HERE!

Spray your cutting with water to keep the top moist.

2 Take the base of your lettuce and put it into the bowl. Only the very bottom of the plant should be covered by water, not the cut-off top of your lettuce.

Change the water in the bowl every couple of days.

3 Put the bowl in a sunny spot—your lettuce needs to get as much light as possible each day. In a few days you should see leaves growing from the base.

A window box or pot makes a great home for lettuce!

4 Once you can see the leaves thickening and growing you can plant your lettuce in soil. Plant it so that only the leaves are showing. Now watch it grow to full size!

Pimp up your
Pesto

For a pesto that still packs a punch, swap the traditional basil and pine nuts for **TIRED NUTS OR SEEDS, CARROT LEAVES,** *or* **LEFTOVER PARSLEY STALKS.**

MAKES ABOUT ⅔ CUP

2 cloves garlic, roughly chopped

1⅔ cups basil leaves, roughly chopped

⅓ cup pine nuts

1 tbsp apple cider vinegar

¼ cup olive oil

salt and freshly ground black pepper, to taste

FIRST **MAKE THE BASE**

1 Place the garlic, basil, pine nuts, and vinegar in a food processor and blend until combined.

2 With the motor running, slowly drizzle the olive oil into the pesto until combined. You may need to stop the machine occasionally to push the mixture down with a spatula.

3 Season with salt and pepper to taste.

4 Store in an airtight container in the fridge for up to 1 week.

Super *tip*
Swap parsley stalks for wilting herbs such as mint or cilantro.

TIRED NUTS OR SEEDS

Swap the pine nuts for ⅓ **cup tired nuts or seeds**, such as walnuts or pumpkin seeds. Blend them in the food processor before adding the other ingredients, then add one extra tbsp vinegar and an extra 2–4 tbsp olive oil. Adjust the oil as needed to get the right consistency.

CARROT LEAVES

Swap the basil for **2oz (65g) thoroughly washed carrot leaves**, plus an extra tbsp vinegar and an extra 2–4 tbsp olive oil. Carrot leaves are less juicy than basil, so adjust the amount of olive oil accordingly.

LEFTOVER PARSLEY STALKS

Swap the basil for **2oz (65g) leftover parsley stalks**, plus an extra tbsp vinegar and an extra 2–4 tbsp olive oil.

Tired nuts or seeds

Carrot leaves

Leftover parsley stalks

Bananas

*Is your fruit bowl **BURSTING** with **BANANAS?** Don't let them turn black and end up in the trash. Try some of these **AWESOME IDEAS** to make the most of **EVERY BIT** of this fabulous fruit.*

PERFECT PEEL!

Freeze banana peels to save them for use in baking cakes (see recipe p.59).

BUTTER IT UP

Squash overripe bananas onto toast or rolls as a sweet swap for butter.

BANANAMOLE

Mash up overripe bananas with avocado to bulk out your guacamole, or even try replacing all the avocado with banana in your favorite guacamole recipe for a sweeter alternative.

FROZEN TREAT

Peel bananas, break into chunks, and freeze on a tray. Save in a freezer bag, and add to smoothies as needed.

BANANA CHIPS

Slice up bananas that are fairly firm and use them to make chips. Make sure your slices are the same thickness, brush them with lemon juice, and place them on a baking tray. Bake at 225°F (110°C) for 2–3 hours until brown. Let them cool and crisp.

MAKE IT MOIST

Add a ripe banana peel to the bottom of a roasting pan to help keep meat moist and tender while it cooks.

BANANA ICE CREAM

This easy-to-make but utterly delicious frozen treat makes a great healthy and vegan alternative to ice cream. Keep it simple with just one ingredient—a banana—or add any of your favorite flavorings, such as berries or cocoa.

1 Peel a banana—just use more bananas if you want to make a batch of ice cream—and cut into chunks.

2 Freeze the pieces for at least 2 hours, then blend in a food processor until smooth. (Try adding cocoa powder at this stage for chocolate-flavored "ice cream.")

3 You can eat the ice cream right away or transfer to an airtight container and freeze it again to firm it up.

Banana ice cream

Love your leftovers...
Potatoes

Do your leftover potatoes leave you feeling as cold as yesterday's SIDE DISH? Try these tips, and soon you'll be MAKING OVER your mashed potatoes and REVIVING your roasts!

Mashed

Shepherd's pie

TASTY TOPPING

Try using mashed potatoes as a topping for pies instead of pastry. Spread the potato mixture over your filling and place it in the oven until warmed through and browned on top.

Fishcakes

POTATO PATTIES

Recycle your leftover mashed potatoes into potato cakes by mixing an egg with the mixture and adding some herbs. Form into patties or balls, and fry each side in a little oil until warmed through and crispy on the outside. Try adding cooked fish or bacon into the mix for extra flavor.

ADD THICKNESS

Mashed potatoes make a great alternative to cornflour when it comes to thickening up your sauces, soups, or stews. Blend your leftover mashed potatoes in a food processor until smooth—you may need to add a little milk or some of the dish you are thickening. Once it is smooth, gradually stir into your soup or sauce until it reaches your desired consistency.

Blending in mashed potatoes thickens soup

Potato and bacon soup

Boiled

Roasted

Baked

SUPER SALAD

Boiled potatoes can be reworked into tasty potato salad. Cut the potatoes into bite-size pieces and mix with mayonnaise, natural yogurt, boiled egg, peas, herbs, and chopped radishes (or whatever vegetables you have on hand)!

Fresh herbs liven up potato salad

JUST ADD EGGS

Leftover roasted potatoes make a great addition to a frittata (see pp.30–31) or Spanish omelette. Whisk 3 or 4 eggs with a little water and seasoning. Fry a sliced onion in a little oil over medium heat until golden brown. Slice your potatoes, then add them to the pan. Pour in the egg mixture and reduce heat. Let the omelette cook for about 12 minutes.

Frittata

STUFFED SPUDS

Give baked potatoes a new lease on life by mixing up the flesh with flavorful fillings. Slice your baked potatoes in half and scoop out the flesh. Place it in a bowl with fillings of your choice. Mix it all together and season to taste. Stuff the filling into the potato skin, sprinkle on some grated cheese, and bake in the oven until warmed through and the top has browned.

Crispy, golden topping

Cheese and bacon

Creative
Chips

Transform **POTATO PEELINGS** *or* **OLD VEGETABLES** *into these delicious chips. A healthy snack from leftover vegetables!*

SERVES 2

1¾oz (50g) potato peel from around 2 large potatoes

½ tbsp olive oil

a generous pinch of chili powder

½ tsp sweet smoked paprika powder

¼ tsp salt

freshly ground black pepper, to taste

¾ cup kale leaves

FIRST MAKE THE BASE

1 Preheat the oven to 300°F (150°C) and line 2–3 baking sheets with parchment paper.

2 Place the potato peel in a mixing bowl with half of the oil, spices, salt, and pepper. Using your hands (wear gloves if necessary), gently rub the peel until it is completely coated with oil and spices. Set aside.

3 Using a sharp knife, remove the tough, woody kale stems and roughly chop the leaves into bite-sized pieces.

4 Place the kale in a mixing bowl with the remaining oil, spices, salt, and pepper. Gently rub the kale for 1–2 minutes until it is completely coated and starting to soften.

5 Spread the potato peel and kale thinly on separate baking sheets in single, even layers. Set the kale sheet aside.

6 Place the potato peel in the oven and leave to roast for 25 minutes. After 10 minutes, add the kale sheet and continue roasting for the remaining 15 minutes, or until crisp. Watch carefully to ensure they don't burn.

7 Remove the chips from the oven and leave on the sheets for a few minutes to crisp up before eating.

8 The chips are best eaten within a few hours, but can be stored in an airtight container for 1–2 days. Re-crisp them in the oven at a low temperature for 3–4 minutes.

Super tip
Combine all the veggies to create a rainbow of flavors and colors.

SWEET POTATO AND POTATO PEEL CHIPS

Swap the kale for the peel of 2 large sweet potatoes—about 1¾oz (50g). Combine with the regular potato peel and season as per the recipe. Roast both for 25 minutes, or until crisp.

TIRED PARSNIP AND POTATO PEEL CHIPS

Swap the kale for 1 parsnip—about 3½oz (100g). Slice very thinly either with a mandolin or a vegetable peeler, including tops and tails. Season, spread thinly on a baking sheet, and roast for around 35 minutes, or until crisp. Thicker slices may need an extra 5 minutes, but watch carefully to ensure they don't burn. Add the potato peel sheet to the oven for the last 25 minutes.

TIRED BEET AND POTATO PEEL CHIPS

Swap the kale for 1 beet—about 3½oz (100g). Slice very thinly either with a mandolin or a vegetable peeler, including tops and tails. Season, spread thinly on a baking sheet, and roast for around 35 minutes, or until crisp. Thicker slices may need an extra 5 minutes, but watch carefully to ensure they don't burn. Add the potato peel sheet to the oven for the last 25 minutes.

Everything
in its place!

Knowing whether to put your food in the PANTRY, FREEZER, or FRIDGE will help it last longer and reduce waste. LABEL FOODS so you know what will spoil when. Track what you use and what you waste.

Fridge

Check up on your refrigerated foods regularly and move older foods to the front so that you use them up before newer foods. Label anything that is going off as a reminder to use it soon! Knowing exactly what is in your fridge means you can avoid buying duplicates.

The warmest part of your fridge is the door, so use it for items that are less sensitive to temperature. Bottles or jars of condiments and cartons of juice do well here.

The top shelf of your fridge has the most consistent temperature and anything that is ready to eat, like dairy products and cooked meat, should be kept here.

Don't store cheese in plastic wrap—it needs to breathe. It will last longer in wax paper.

For freshness, keep red spices, like paprika and chilli, in the fridge in airtight tins or jars.

Raw foods that will need to be cooked, like meat and fish, should be stored on the bottom shelf of the fridge so that they can't drip onto anything.

Peppers and lettuce are best kept in a plastic bag in the salad drawer.

Super *tip*

Put mushrooms in a paper bag in the fridge to stop them going slimy.

Super *tip*

To stop potatoes, garlic, and onions sprouting keep them in paper bags in a dark, dry place.

Pantry

Your pantry is the best place for jars of dried foods, and bottles of oil or vinegar that don't need to be chilled but do need to be cool, dry, and dark.

Freezer

The golden rule for freezing food is to label everything! On the label, make sure you include what kind of food it is and the date you made or bought it. Arrange your freezer so that the label faces outward with older foods toward the front. This means that you won't have to rummage around and mess up all your neat work.

To stop brown sugar going hard, keep it in an airtight container and add moist foods like a slice of bread or marshmallows for 1–2 days. The sugar will soften as it soaks up any moisture.

Vaccuum sealing leftovers before you freeze them can save valuable freezer space and it helps prevent freezer-burn. Another waste-saving tip is to freeze food by serving size so you only defrost what you need and don't end up with leftovers.

Arrange your pantry by grouping like items together so that you can find them quickly and keep an eye on what you have in stock. It's useful to label anything that is coming to the end of its shelf-life and needs to be used soon. Storing items in clear, glass, airtight containers allows you to see exactly how much you have.

Shop smart!

*Stop before you shop! Take time to plan **WHAT** you need, **WHERE** you should buy it, and **HOW MUCH** to get in one go—without wasting it.*

LEARN TO LiST

A shopping list is essential for making sure that you buy only what you need when you need it. Start by making your meal plan for the week (see pp.14–15) and checking what ingredients you already have in your kitchen. List anything that you'll need along with the quantities required. Once you're out shopping, make sure you stick to your list and don't let tempting special offers drag you off-plan!

Build your list from your meal plan.

WHERE TO SHOP

Supermarkets are convenient for buying everything under one roof, but your local farmers' market has its advantages. Local produce is fresher as it has traveled less far and it comes with less packaging—you can even hand back any ties or bands on the produce to the stallholder. So make an effort to buy your perishable goods locally at the market. They often sell imperfect vegetables that supermarkets refuse, so you may also find that shopping here is cheaper.

Fruit and vegetable market

Don't forget your reusable bag when you head to the store!

BARGAIN BEWARE!

Don't be tempted by what might look like great bargain buys. Shops discount fresh produce that is near or at its use-by date but unless you're sure you will use it all right away, you will end up wasting it. Try to buy loose fruit and vegetables where you can and select the exact number you need rather than cheap multipacks, or you may end up throwing away more than you use!

Bags of salad go off quickly, so note the dates.

Pick the exact amount of veggies you need.

BUYING iN BULK

Buying large quantities of food at one time is cheaper, reduces packaging, and the number of shopping trips you make. But only bulk-buy foods that will keep long enough for you to use them. Good foods to buy in bulk include: dried beans, rice, oats, pasta, nuts, dried fruit and condiments you use often. When decanting bulk buys don't top-up containers, make sure you remove any remaining food first and put it back on the top so that it gets used next.

Super tip

Clearly label the containers you store your bulk buys in with the use-by dates.

Store all your bulk buys in airtight jars for freshness.

Brown rice   Buckwheat   Lentils   Slivered almonds

Peanuts   Hazelnuts   Almonds   Raisins   Brazil nuts   Walnuts   Dried figs   Dates

Go-nuts
Granola Bars

*Add a fruity twist to your granola bars with **OVERRIPE BERRIES,** CITRUS PEEL, or even **LEFTOVER PULP** from your juicer.*

SERVES 12–16

½ cup coconut oil

½ cup honey or rice syrup

⅔ cup nut or seed butter

1¼ cups rolled oats

3½oz (100g) slivered almonds

1¾oz (50g) ground almonds

1 tbsp ground cinnamon

3½oz (100g) mixed dried fruit, such as dates, raisins, figs, or goji berries, chopped

1½ cups mixed seeds, such as pumpkin, sunflower, chia, sesame, or hemp

FIRST MAKE THE BASE

1 Preheat the oven to 350°F (180°C) and line a 12 x 8in (30 x 20cm) baking sheet with parchment paper.

2 Gently heat the oil, honey, and nut or seed butter in a pan until combined.

3 Mix all the other ingredients in a large bowl.

4 Pour the honey mixture over the oats and stir until thoroughly combined.

5 Turn the mixture into the baking sheet and level out, pressing down firmly with the back of a spoon. Bake for 25–30 minutes until golden brown.

6 Leave the granola bars on the sheet on a wire rack to cool completely before slicing.

7 Store in an airtight container in the fridge for up to 1 week, or freeze for up to 1 month.

NOW ZERO-WASTE IT!

OVERRIPE BERRIES

Heat 5½oz (150g) **berries**, such as **blueberries or raspberries**, and **1 tbsp water** in a saucepan over medium heat for about 5 minutes, until soft. Mash with a fork, then add the oil, honey, and nut or seed butter.

SATSUMA, TANGERINE, OR MANDARIN PEEL

Add the **finely chopped peel** of a piece of **citrus fruit** (about 2 tbsp) at step 2.

LEFTOVER JUICING PULP

There are endless flavor possibilities from whatever you used in your juice! Add 5½oz (150g) juicing pulp to the honey mixture at step 1, combine, then continue as per the recipe.

Super tip

Eat them raw! Instead of baking, freeze for 1 hour, then store in the fridge.

I'm raw!

One-meal wonder

Find out just how far **ONE MEAL** *can go with these awesome ideas for making the* **MOST** *of your* **ROAST.**

Sunday:
The **big** dinner

You've cooked a roasted chicken dinner. What can you do with the leftover meat, potatoes, and accompanying vegetables? And how long will they keep before they spoil? Cooked meat keeps for about 3 to 4 days, and vegetables keep for up to 5 days if refrigerated. Store both in airtight containers in the fridge.

Roasted chicken dinner

Monday:

Lunch
VEGETABLE FRITTERS

Use up some leftover cooked vegetables by shredding them into a bowl with a little grated cheese. Season and mix well. Stir in an egg and combine. Fry spoonfuls of the mix in olive oil over medium heat for a couple of minutes on each side or until crisp.

Dinner
ROASTED CHICKEN STIR-FRY

Add leftover roasted chicken to your stir-fry mix. Make sure it is completely heated through before serving.

Tuesday:

Lunch
SALAD WITH POTATO CROUTONS

Give texture to your salad by adding roasted potato croutons. Simply take the potatoes out of the fridge and allow them to come back to room temperature—or refry for extra crunch. Then crumble them over your salad.

Dinner
CHICKEN TACOS

Shred your leftover chicken and fry it in a little oil along with taco spices and your choice of seasoning. Warm tortillas in a pan and spoon in your spicy chicken. Add toppings, such as cheese, sour cream, beans, salsa, and lettuce.

Wednesday:

Lunch
BUBBLE & SQUEAK

To make this popular British dish, mix leftover vegetables in a bowl and season. Heat some butter or oil in a pan and fry the mixture over medium heat for about 10 minutes, turning frequently, until crisp and browned. Serve with scrambled eggs and grilled tomatoes.

Dinner
CHICKEN, VEGETABLE, & PASTA BAKE

Stir bite-size chunks of leftover roasted chicken into your mix for a vegetable and pasta bake before putting it in the oven.

10 foods you didn't know you could... FREEZE

NUTS

With their high oil content, nuts such as pecans, almonds, and walnuts are prone to going rancid, which can be a problem when buying in bulk. Freeze them—either in their shells or shelled—and they will last at least twice as long.

KEEPS FOR
1-2
YEARS

OPENED WINE

Freeze any leftover wine in ice cube trays, transfer the cubes to freezer bags, and then add them into sauces, stews, or risottos straight from the freezer.

KEEPS FOR
6
MONTHS

HARD CHEESES

Never let an old block of cheese molder away at the back of the fridge again! It's best to grate it first, so that you can grab handfuls as you need them, and store it in an airtight bag or container.

KEEPS FOR
6
MONTHS

FRESH HERBS

If a recipe calls for just a sprig or two of fresh herbs, what do you do with the rest of the bunch? Freeze it of course! Place unneeded fresh herbs in an ice cube tray, cover with a little water, leave to freeze, then transfer to freezer bags.

KEEPS FOR
6
MONTHS

MASHED POTATOES

If you've got a bag of potatoes past their prime, make a large batch of mashed potato and freeze individual portions for later. Use the same method for sweet potato or rutabagas, too.

KEEPS FOR
2
MONTHS

Making friends with your **FREEZER** is a great way to avoid food waste. If you're buying in **BULK** to cut down on **PACKAGING**, freezing your produce will ensure it doesn't go bad before you can use it.

Super tip

Glass jars are great for freezing foods and can be recycled (unlike plastic bags or wrap). Leave space for the contents to expand.

EGGS

You can store raw egg in the freezer—but not whole eggs, which may expand and crack. Either whisk in a bowl and pour the mixture into an ice cube tray or, if you're a good baker, why not freeze the whites and yolks separately?

KEEPS FOR **1** YEAR

COOKED PASTA

Freezing is a great way to preserve any leftover cooked pasta. Make sure you cook it al dente, otherwise it may go mushy when you defrost it.

KEEPS FOR **2** MONTHS

CAKE

You can freeze cake as long as it doesn't have any icing, filling, or decoration. Either freeze it whole or cut it into slices and store them individually. Freezing cake also reduces the crumbs around the edges, making it easier to ice.

KEEPS FOR **6** MONTHS

UNCOOKED BROWN RICE

Brown rice has a higher natural oil content than white rice, so its shelf life is much shorter. The simple solution? Freeze it in a sealed, airtight container.

KEEPS FOR **6** MONTHS

DICED VEGETABLES

Dice fresh onions, peppers, or chiles, and freeze them flat in freezer bags. Press "score lines" into the bags before they have fully frozen so that you can break off individual portions.

KEEPS FOR **1** MONTH

Fruity Cake

Choose **BANANA PEELS, PINEAPPLE CORES,** *or* **NUT MILK PULP** *to turn up the flavor in this wonderful waste-free treat.*

MAKES 8–12 SLICES

¼ cup coconut oil

½ cup maple syrup

1 tsp vanilla extract

1 cup chickpea, brown rice, or whole-wheat flour

5oz (140g) ground almonds

1 tbsp baking powder

1 tsp cinnamon

⅓ cup walnuts, chopped

9oz (250g) mixed dried fruit, such as apricots, prunes, raisins, figs, or dates, chopped

3 eggs, separated

½ cup fresh orange juice (about 2 large oranges)

1 tbsp flax seeds

FIRST MAKE THE BASE

1 Preheat the oven to 350°F (180°C), and grease and line a 8in (20cm) round cake pan, or 2lb (900g) loaf pan.

2 Place the coconut oil, syrup, and vanilla in a small saucepan. Melt over medium heat, then set aside to cool.

3 In a large mixing bowl, combine the flour, almonds, baking powder, cinnamon, walnuts, and dried fruit.

4 Separate the egg yolks from the whites. Whisk the whites until they form soft peaks, and set aside.

5 Add the orange juice to the cooled syrup mixture, then gently beat in the egg yolks.

6 Pour the syrup mix into the flour mixture and stir until thoroughly combined. Very gently, fold in the egg whites with a spatula.

7 Pour the cake mix into the pan. Level out and sprinkle with flax seeds.

8 Bake the cake for 50–60 minutes, or until golden brown, firm to the touch, and a skewer inserted into the center comes out clean.

9 Leave the cake to cool in the pan for 5 minutes. Then place on a wire rack, and allow to cool completely before serving. Store in an airtight container for up to 1 week.

Super tip
Save the eggshells to make Eggshell Powder on p.22.

NOW **ZERO-WASTE IT!**

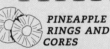

BANANA PEEL

Swap the dried fruit and juice for 9oz (250g) topped, tailed, and roughly chopped ripe **banana peels** (about 4–6 peels). Whizz in a food processor or blender with **½ cup water** until smooth and dark. Combine with the syrup mixture and egg yolks at step 5.

PINEAPPLE RINGS AND CORES

Replace the mixed dried fruit with about 5½oz (150g) **thinly sliced, skinned pineapple rings, with cores**. Replace the orange juice with **pineapple juice** and omit the flax seeds. Put the rings at the bottom of the baking tin and pour the cake mixture on top. Serve the cake upside-down with the baked pineapple on top.

LEFTOVER NUT MILK PULP

Swap the ground almonds for an **equal amount of very thoroughly squeezed nut milk pulp**, such as almond or hazelnut pulp (see below), and continue as per the recipe.

Nut milk

To make nut milk, soak **1 cup nuts** overnight in double their volume of water, then drain and rinse. Place in a blender or processor with **3¼ cups filtered water** and blend for 30–60 seconds. Strain the milk through muslin into a bowl.

Know when to throw: fruit and vegetables

Learn when your FRUIT and VEGETABLES can be RESCUED or when they are past the point of no return and destined for COMPOSTING.

VILE VEGETABLES!

Take a look at your vegetables. If they are a bit dry or limp, they can be rescued. If they are mushy, slimy, or discolored, they are rotten, and you should discard them. Some vegetables behave differently when they go bad.

LOSE THAT BRUISE

While mushiness and wrinkles signal that your fruit is no longer good to eat, bruised fruit can be salvaged. Bruises are caused by damage in transport or handling rather than spoilage. Simply cut away the bruised part and then enjoy the rest of the fruit.

Cut away bruise

Celery becomes white and hollow

Eggplants toughen up and skin dimples

Asparagus tips go soft and turn black

Bad apples may smell sour

FOUL FRUIT!

To check whether soft fruits can be saved, you need to examine their skins. The skins of fruits like apricots, plums, and grapes should be smooth, not wrinkled or peeling away.

When fruit is going bad, it tends to start smelling unpleasant, so ditch any fruits with a foul odor.

Give hard fruits, such as melons, a squeeze. They should be quite firm with no squashy areas. Check the skin for any dark patches, which develop when the fruit is going bad.

Fresh apricots have smooth skin

Melons should have no squashy patches

SAVE YOUR GREENS

Leafy greens can wilt within a couple of days, but this doesn't always mean you have to throw them away. Soak stems in warm water for about 10–15 minutes. If this doesn't revive them, put them in the compost.

REVIVED

COMPOST

61

Love your leftovers...
Rice

COLD RICE

Treat your rice right and don't let it end up in the TRASH. With a little care, you can reuse it in some of these TASTY DISHES.

YES YOU CAN

REHEAT RICE

Worried about reheating rice? It is safe to heat up leftover rice the next day so long as you have kept it in the fridge and not left it out overnight. Once you have cooked rice, you should chill it as soon as possible and keep it cool in the fridge until you want to use it.

PERFECT PUDDING

Leftover cooked rice is perfect for rice pudding. Cover the rice with milk in a pot and stir over medium heat until it boils, then reduce the heat. Sweeten with honey or maple syrup. Add more milk if you like your pudding less solid. Keep stirring until the rice is soft and you have the consistency desired.

+ sugar & cinnamon

+ fruit & spices

+ fruit compote

SIMPLE SALAD

You can add pretty much anything to your chilled leftover rice to make a delicious salad. Try mixing in leftover roasted vegetables, tuna, or cooked beans for a quick and healthy lunch. Include some chopped fresh herbs and add a squeeze of lemon juice to give it a boost of flavor.

CRISP CRUST

Cooked rice (shortgrain works best) makes a great alternative to a pastry for crusty toppings or bases for pies and quiches. Mix your leftover rice with some grated cheese and egg white, then press together to form a crust. Or spray a pie pan with oil, and press the mix on to the bottom and sides of the pan. Bake in the oven until firm, then cool before filling.

crispy rice and parmesan base

Tomato and Dijon tart

GET STUFFED

Try stuffing vegetables—such as bell peppers, zucchini, or large tomatoes—with your leftover rice. Slice the top off the peppers (keep them to use as lids once they are stuffed) and remove the seeds. Scoop out zucchini or tomato flesh and chop it up. Mix it with the rice, some herbs, feta cheese, and seasoning before spooning the mixture into the vegetable. Roast the stuffed vegetables in a little olive oil for 20–30 minutes at 325°F (160°C).

Stuffed peppers

stringy mozzarella oozes in the middle

Arancini

RISOTTO BALLS

Use up leftover risotto by making arancini (fried rice balls). A gooey mozzarella center is a must, so cut some into chunks. Take your chilled risotto and roll it in your hands to form a ball about 2in (5cm) across. Poke a hole in the center, then push in some mozzarella and any other fillings of your choice. Next, roll the ball in some flour, dip it in beaten egg, and coat with breadcrumbs. Fry the ball in olive oil until crisp and golden.

Rice salad

Breadbox
clear-out

Bread is one of the foods we **THROW AWAY** *most. Buck the trend by trying out some of these tasty tips.*

BREAD REVIVAL

Bring bread that is past its date back to life by freshening it up in the oven. Preheat your oven to 300°F (150°C), then sprinkle the crust of your bread with a little water. Bake the bread for about 8–10 minutes, depending on the size of the loaf, or until warmed through and the crust is crisped.

SOAK IT UP

Stale bread makes a handy sponge for drawing up excess fat. Put a slice on top of oily gravy, soups, or stews for a few seconds and it will soak up any unwanted grease. Discard the bread once it's soaked.

FRY IT UP

An easy way to use up dry bread is to simply fry or toast it. For a tasty brunch, try making French toast. Whisk an egg, a few drops of vanilla extract, and a pinch of cinnamon in a shallow dish. Next, stir in a little milk. Dip the stale bread into the mixture, making sure both sides are coated. Fry both sides in a little oil or butter over medium heat until golden brown.

BREADCRUMBS

While fresh bread is not good for making breadcrumbs, older, dry bread is perfect. Avoid bread that is truly stale, as it will make stale-tasting crumbs.

1 Make your breadcrumbs in a food processor or use a grater. Simply cut off the crusts then process or grate the bread into crumbs. Breadcrumbs made in a food processor are usually finer and more uniform in size than the grated ones.

2 Freeze your breadcrumbs—put them into an airtight container in the freezer. They should keep for up to 2 months.

3 Use your breadcrumbs to make everything from meatballs to veggie sausages, or mix with cheese, herbs, and spices to create a tasty topping for vegetables or chicken.

CRUNCHY CROUTONS

Use stale bread to make croutons. Slice and remove crusts, then brush both sides with olive oil. Break or slice into bite-size chunks or cubes. Bake in the oven at 350°F (180°C) for about 20 minutes or until golden brown. Let cool before adding to soups or salads. Croutons can be stored in an airtight container for up to two weeks or frozen for up to a month.

EXTRA THICK

Add bulk and texture to soups by adding stale bread. Cut the crusts off the bread and tear it into chunks. Add the chunks to your soup and simmer for a few minutes to let the bread break down. Your soup should thicken up instantly.

Waste-not Want-not Muffins

Choose **TIRED SWEET POTATO, BEET,** *or* **ZUCCHINI,** *and add* **WILTING HERBS** *to make these muffins your own.*

SERVES 12

½ cup coconut or olive oil, plus extra for greasing

1 cup chickpea, buckwheat, brown rice, or whole-wheat flour

1 tbsp baking powder

½ tsp salt

2 eggs

1 cup milk, either nut or dairy

2 tbsp finely chopped parsley

2 scallions, including green tops, finely chopped (about 3–4 tbsp)

freshly ground black pepper, to taste

1⅓ cups carrot, grated (about 2 carrots)

½ cup cheese such as Cheddar, feta, or Parmesan, grated or crumbled (optional)

FIRST **MAKE THE BASE**

1 Preheat the oven to 400°F (200°C) and grease a 12-hole muffin pan with a little oil.

2 If using coconut oil, melt it in a saucepan over medium heat, and set aside to cool.

3 Combine the flour, baking powder, and salt in a mixing bowl, then set aside.

4 Lightly whisk the eggs and milk together, then stir in the parsley and onions. Add the oil and season with pepper to taste.

5 Pour the egg mixture into the flour mixture and stir until thoroughly combined, then fold in the carrot and cheese, if using.

6 Divide the mixture evenly between the muffin holes and bake for 15–20 minutes until golden brown and a skewer inserted into the center comes out clean.

7 Leave the muffins to cool in the tray for 5 minutes, then run a knife around each muffin to loosen before turning out onto a wire rack.

8 These muffins are best eaten warm, but can be stored in an airtight container in the fridge for up to 1 week. Reheat in the oven at 300°F (150°C) for 5 minutes before serving, if desired.

TIRED SWEET POTATO AND THYME

Swap the carrot for grated sweet potato (with skin on), and the parsley for thyme, or any other wilting herbs that need using up.

- - - - - - - -

TIRED BEET AND CILANTRO

Swap the carrot for grated beet (with skin on), and the parsley for cilantro, or any other wilting herbs that need using up.

- - - - - - - -

TIRED ZUCCHINI AND MINT

Swap the carrot for grated zucchini (with skin on), and the parsley for mint, or any other wilting herbs that need using up.

Super *tip*
keeping the skin on your veggies adds extra nutrients.

It's more than food!

Think beyond leftovers and vegetable peelings—you may waste more than just food in your kitchen. From **FOIL** *and* **FOOD WRAPS** *to* **PLASTIC BAGS** *and* **PACKAGING,** *here are some tips to cut your nonfood kitchen waste.*

FOILED!

There's no need to use disposable aluminum foil, when there are reusable alternatives. Try silicone baking mats instead of foil sheets. If you do use them, clean aluminum foil wrap and trays can usually be recycled.

ZAP IT!

Don't toss your old kitchen sponges. Revive them and kill any lingering bacteria by soaking them and zapping them in the microwave for a couple of minutes. Don't attempt this with sponges that contain any metal, such as heavy-duty scourers.

Foil trays

Kitchen sponge

ON TAP

Don't buy bottled water when you can drink water from your kitchen faucet. Use glass bottles or jugs if you prefer your water chilled from the fridge. If you are concerned about water quality in your area, consider investing in a countertop filter.

Foil sheet

GADGET ADDICT

Think before you buy the latest kitchen gadgets—do you really need it and will you use it? For example, spiralizers are great fun but your vegetable peeler can produce similar results.

Use a peeler to make vegetable ribbons

Zucchini ribbons

IT'S A COVER UP

Avoid plastic wrap by making your own reusable cloth covers for jars, plates, and bowls. You can use old cotton shirts or sheets to make these truly zero-waste! Simply cut circles out of the cloth, making sure they are around 2in (5cm) larger in diameter than the items you want to cover. Then gather the edge and stitch in some elastic. Now you're covered!

This is the size of the top of the jar or bowl

Add 5cm (2in) extra all around the edge

food cover

BULK UP!

Buying large quantities of food, such as dry goods like rice and flour that you can store, reduces packaging overall. This works out cheaper so it is easy on your pocket and it means fewer shopping trips, saving you time! Look out for stores that specialize in bulk buying, allowing you to bring your own reusable containers to fill with food.

Reusable containers mean less packaging

A fabric bag can be used over and over

Rice

IN THE BAG

Ditch wasteful plastic grocery bags and replace them with durable fabric tote bags. To avoid forgetting them, keep your reusable bags by the door, in the car, or in a fold-up mini shopping bag in your pocket or handbag.

Grow it, don't throw it: potatoes

Did you know that you can GROW your own POTATOES from OLD SPUDS and the SCRAPS that you usually throw away? Follow these simple steps and you'll be HARVESTING SPUDS for months to come!

1 Check over your old potatoes and pick out some that have two or three good "eyes" on them.

Eye

CHOP HERE!

2 Cut your old potatoes in half or trim scraps into pieces that are around 2in (5cm) across.

Make sure each half has one or two eyes

3 Leave your potato halves or scraps out to dry, preferably overnight, or until they are dry to the touch.

Turn the potato around so the eyes are on top

4 Plant the potato pieces about 8in (20cm) deep in soil with the eyes facing up. Leave around 1ft (30cm) between your potatoes.

1ft (30cm) between each potato

shoots will begin to grow from the eyes

5 In a few weeks' time you should see your potato plant start to grow!

New potatoes are ready in 10–12 weeks, larger varieties in 20–26 weeks

Index

Acknowledgments

Kate Turner has been creating deliciously healthy food for herself and her family for years. She has a degree in health sciences and is a recipe writer, magazine contributor, and author. Her DK publications include *Energy Bites, Superfood Breakfasts,* and *Power Bowls.* Kate shares ideas about food and family life on her blog **homegrownkate.com**.